Hidden

poems by

Sarah Leamy

Finishing Line Press
Georgetown, Kentucky

Hidden

Copyright © 2021 by Sarah Leamy
ISBN 978-1-64662-474-4 First Edition
All rights reserved under International and Pan-American Copyright Conventions. No part of this book may be reproduced in any manner whatsoever without written permission from the publisher, except in the case of brief quotations embodied in critical articles and reviews.

Publisher: Leah Huete de Maines
Editor: Christen Kincaid
Cover Art: Sarah Leamy
Author Photo: Sarah Leamy, © Sarah Leamy 2020
Cover Design: Elizabeth Maines McCleavy

Printed in the USA on acid-free paper.
Order online: www.finishinglinepress.com
also available on amazon.com

Author inquiries and mail orders:
Finishing Line Press
P. O. Box 1626
Georgetown, Kentucky 40324
U. S. A.

Table of Contents

Guilt 1

The Old Story

The New Neighborhood 5

How to Act 6

As If 7

Out 8

Old School Scars 9

Flash Flood 10

I'm Addicted 11

Old School Secrets 12

A Heavy Drizzle 13

It Was Not Hard 14

Compare and Contrast 17

Still Nervous 18

Fear of Assimilation 19

Last Chance 20

Broken 21

Heading Out 22

You Stole His Bike 23

White Lies and Alcohol 25

Epilogue

Down in the Dirt 29

CODA

Guilt

The traffic cop busted me:
No driver's license. No registration. No insurance. No helmet.

He took me, handcuffed, in the back of his shiny new Ford to the
station on the east side of town.
The interview room was upstairs, overlooking two-lane highways and
bland suburban houses, lined up like nice little white boys waiting
for their girl scouts to bring cookies. Such an orderly world, nothing
hidden there.

I'd had one call to make bail.
The question stumped me.
Who could I, should I call? My lover, Clara?
But what would it cost?

Clara had gone off for the day with my neighbor,
her husband,
Henry. They were getting back together. I wasn't meant to know.

Riding Henry's BMW GS 850 had been so worth it though, I
confessed to the booking officer
who then called Henry and
                              we all paid for it.

THE OLD STORY

The New Neighborhood

When I walked the dog around the block, I was too aware of being watched. Henry lived on the corner in the house with the wooden porch that I'd sat upon drinking his chilled beer whilst chatting that first evening after I'd moved in and Clara sat next to him on the swing, and we'd all talked, them asking how long was I staying, a month to month I'd said, unsure of my plans and switching topics to my research, his new motorcycle and lakes and literature and her work at the library and we ate strawberries, drank and laughed and chatted into the late night, easy company, and I don't like to think about how much that first night in town affected me. I couldn't talk to my friends about it as they'd have said, *really? again?* and they'd shake their heads but they didn't know about how less than a week later, she took me to their upstairs bed with fans flicking warm air across sultry afternoon sweaty backs and it was all so predictable, a midlife crisis for her or was it mine —another straight woman attracted to my so-called boyish good looks, and well, I need to air out my dirty laundry and the stickyslick sheets covered with the scent of Clara and I remember wanting to text her, say—come over, I'm done with the dog walk—and give me more time to breathe you in, and please, let's hold on to another fivefastsmitten moment before I fuck it all up and have to leave but instead, walking home alone, I put the phone away, sighing because I'd flipped through my phone to linger over candid photos of other lovers, reminding me how my life stories repeat and I wondered if this time, the husband wouldn't need to know.

How to act when you have a crush on the woman next door even though you should know better because she's straight and you're not

Go see her often at work. Stop by the library. Get a new card. Say hello. Ask her questions. Listen. Start telling stories. Make her laugh. Repeat. Try not to light up when she smiles back at you. Try not to grin when she makes you laugh. Suddenly realize that it's been a week already and so one day, you stop by and sit next to her as she helps you on the computer and you both look at the screen and you ask sensible questions that you probably could have worked out on your own but it's so much better to brainstorm with another. Talk about the weather. Talk about dogs. Introduce her to your girl. Tell her that you were thinking of going to the lake for a swim and maybe she'd like to go with you and she gives you her number and says yes maybe but then no. But the next day she texts you. And it's like you're fifteen but without the shitty big brothers pulling a knife on you for looking at their sisters wrong, but it's okay, you're not and what should you do now? Come on, grow up, you tell yourself at four in the morning, wanting to text her back but didn't and so you'd slept badly, words bitten back but come on, honestly, what should you do? Tell her? But she's married with a kid and a husband. Although…maybe I will.

As If

The first time we danced together, Clara was barefoot. It was Henry's 50th birthday and she'd invited the whole block over, even me, the new kid in town, and I wore a blue silk shirt that matched my eyes. She wore a skin tight black dress and yes, all those curves caught my attention. She was now a friendly face in the neighborhood, it's true, but I had barely talked to her outside of the library. I was shy as usual. Her husband, Old Henry, was flirting with Rebecca, a twenty-something poet from New York, showing off his new Beamer bike, cobalt blue it was, gorgeous, I wanted to ride it. Clara stood close to me, and, eyes flashing dark, she grabbed my hand, dragging me onto the wooden floor, so perfectly obvious in her own flirtations as we danced to bad eighties pop music of our teen years. Later that night, she invited me to pop next door and stay for dinner. I turned up at their place just as Henry was heading out on his bike so we nodded but said little else but for, phew, this heat, when's the monsoon coming, who knows, and nice day for a ride, he said with a grin. I went to find Clara and after strolling through kitchen, office, living room and up the stairs I found her in the bathroom, with all those crisp Grecian tiles and mosaics covering curved walls, and the window ledges were full of thick leafy plants, moist from the steamy shower. Water flowed over her tanned shoulders and pale hips and she talked through the fog and came out reaching for a warm towel. I handed one over as she stood in front of me, skin glistening, both of us dripping. She dried off and chatted to me. She reached for nail polish, handed it to me. I unscrewed it and gave it back. No, she said, I want you to paint my nails, and she placed your bare foot on the tub as if she'd been lovers with tomboy dykes all her life.

Out

Dinner had been going so well. Then Clara had pointed to a fresh scab on my right wrist next to an old scar of mine. I flinched and tried to turn away, not knowing which she wanted to ask about, but she took my hands and held me in place. *Remember*, she said, *remember how we were going to start out the way we wanted to go on, that means talking about hard stuff, so go on, tell me, it's okay, I won't judge you. Who cut you?* We stared at my wrist for a moment too long. Awkward. I poured her another glass of the expensive Malbec and slowly, eventually said, *I can't.* Our spaghetti grew colder. She waited for more. I drank more. She didn't. I picked at the pink and green scab, and it fell onto my plate so I ate it. It was crunchy like the pasta. She laughed and reached for me anyway.

Old School Scars

Thumped. Staggered. A smack. Sure sounded solid. Teach him to answer back. The Brother made that cheeky boy loosen his own belt. The Brother, our esteemed Math Teacher, was a fat little bugger with heavy shoulders, double chin, old. He sagged at the knees, shaking at the sight of our Graham, bending over the table with his school trousers down. It's our friend we all felt sorry for, there was nothing we could do for him, Graham, he was one of us wasn't he, with his shirt hanging low over his stained old undies, poor sod. That's the problem though, we didn't say anything, I didn't, only my Harriet of all people, she stood up and yelled at the teacher, telling him it wasn't on, this wasn't the seventies, wasn't some private boys' school, no this wasn't on, she yelled, a looker she was even then, and she's still feisty and grand. The pathetic professor told poor Graham to pull 'em up, sit back down but no more spitting at the girls, right? Graham stood up quietly, nodding shyly at Harriet sitting in the first row. She almost smiled at him but hid behind shaggy hair. Harriet liked Graham. Not me. Not. Me. I'm a girl. She didn't notice girls like me.

Flash flood

Text number 303: I want you.

A few days later, I sat in the library at my favourite desk, the one with a good view, writing my paper but then Henry, that lanky nerd I'd begun to resent, strolled in, carrying a helmet and a packed lunch for Clara and when he saw me, smiled, and asked how my research was going and reluctantly I put down the phone and discussed definitions words literature novels articles websites and critiques and watched as his wife, the librarian walked past,—she of the teasing melting warming breaking spinning texts. Clara headed downstairs ignoring this academic conversation I was caught within. With a grin for me alone, she stepped out of sight as Henry saluted me, saying bye for now, see you later, and he walked away, focused on finding that perfect book to read on his porch, the one that faced mine. I nodded. Another text popped up and I read, 'meet me in the stacks.' In the basement. I did as told. A flash flood drowned the adult I was and left a teenage kid knees exposed in baggy shorts wet crotch and shitfaced grin of how-can-i-be-so-lucky. In rooms crammed with musty books she waits, her moist hands on my lips then hips pulling me in, rocking against her, she bit my neck, rocking me holding me drowning me with those eyes and teeth on skin and her salty grey hair's tied up and with glasses on, she wore a tight little ashen dress with sensible sandals and loose cotton cardigan and the dress pulled up so quick and easy and I reached into her and pulled her to me, filled her up as I drowned.

Text number 304: I'm yours.

I'm addicted

she said
reading whatever she could get
her hands on
books or
bodies
with an overhead fan
cool across my lips
sticky skin
thigh across knee
shades dropped
grandfather clock silent
a dog licked her paw
the clunk of the cat flap
a solitary motorcycle passed
slowly
by as the afternoon dripped
heavy hips
she saw only
what's on the page

Old School Secrets

You. Me. The same. You owe me. Get it yet, you fuckin' dyke? I told you earlier how this would happen, right? I did—we were sitting in the tavern over a pint, chatting again with our families around, all nice and cozy in our old neighborhood, wasn't it? My sister running out all night long with Graham. You following them in the shadows. I remember being a kid, growing up with all us boys, watching you, some freak show you were, trying to be one of us and how one afternoon, you'd asked another stupid question about my sister, trying to be her special friend was it, yes, and you'd pulled out a notepad, a diary, or maybe an address book, and there was no blood inside—yet—I hadn't cut you—and I still don't forget you, a supposed girl, and the choices you've made, the boyfriends left hard and hot, and the kids you'll not have, so you said, begging me to out the knife away, promising to leave her alone, to leave us alone. Oh, you remember me now, you say, you remember our chat that November night in the local down the road from the home you grew up in, the one where you'd hidden from your mom's tantrums and your big brothers' going after you, or me scaring the shit out of you, well, you remember how fast you got out of there—left for the city, all alone? I do and that's why I came to talk to you now you're back, I'll fuck you up if you don't leave my sister alone, you fucking queer, hear me, do you? Because next time, you won't run fast enough. I'll find you. Bleed you dry. I did once. And I will. Again. And again.

A heavy drizzle falls through the leaves

and the dog slept curled up on the front porch and I sprawled on the armchair in shorts, sweatshirt, sandals and damp tee shirt. I drank black coffee, shaking off the night terrors, wondering how long before I messed it up, before I'd be chased out, before I'd get too scared to deal. I stopped thinking, and watched the drips fall from rose bush to grass, getting up to leave a window open for the damn cat in case he decided to come in out of the rain, not that he was even my cat, it's Clara's, a feisty bugger who'd scratched me more than once. As the morning's caffeine kicked in, I decided that it was time for a walk. I grabbed the dog's leash and we headed out into the woods behind us. The cat followed. Then he yelled. And yelled. And so we three turned back and climbed onto the porch once again and the Tom cat sat under a tree in the rain. The dog assumed her usual position, front door, head down, eyes open. She watched a car drive by. The drizzle turned to a heavy rain. The cat jumped onto the deck, yelling for cream. Fine. I poured out the last of the half and half, feeling sorry for the boy, alone on a day like that. Then I sipped my plain coffee. Feet up. Clothes damp. I finally remembered to brush my teeth for when Clara shows up because she would eventually.

It was not hard to tempt her

to claim these short afternoons
two hours at most and she'd
sneak out for
moments
found me waiting
on my porch, reading,
enjoying the
calm of the post storm
 cool breeze and
I claimed that I was
okay with this—for now—
shaking
things up in their
world. Not mine.
Or so I told myself since
for me, it was heated
afternoons together in a
rundown home in the middle of her
town, my boxes still packed, bedding rumpled
and posters tacked to walls,
dirty dishes and half-empty
mugs of old coffee, cooled by
fans in the windows, and my dog's
water bowl on
the wooden floors.
Stay, I said, but didn't mean it
not really,
enjoying her naughty
glee in the 'going
for a walk' and finding me
on the steps, reading poems
and that fake calm hello as we greeted
each other on the porch
before taking
her inside and closing
the doors, before claiming

a few moments to
explore her skin,
wake her up, tease
her thoroughly, before I sent
her back home, to the adult
world of a child needing
dinner, an ex needing
reassurances that she, my lover,
was indeed a mother
was at home on call
all day and all night long
   because he couldn't do it
wouldn't do it
and she did
but the cracks
appeared and the
foundations
slipped in the dampness of
these storms of one
long sweaty
summer together and their home
tilted towards me and away
from him
and while their
kid was off with
 her friends and
her husband was flirting
over a drink with who knows
which young thing
we grabbed an hour
together and
I took my lover
to the lake instead
and in the grey skies and
tepid water we tasted each
other's skin sticky salty and

and holding her up
to the sky and the mirror
of the lake and
we swam in the
afternoon light and
it was enough
—for now—
but I didn't trust it

why would I?

Compare and Contrast

—a hot flash of sweaty skin of belly to tongue, a hot flush of desire as she climbed above me, with my bluewhite butt in the air hands grabbing the pillows as she fucked me from behind and then how only hours later, that same skin was now hidden in boys shorts and tee-shirts like some kind of grad student, asking a librarian for help with a critical thesis and the shine in her eyes made me explode and laughbarksnort, and Clara, with her helpless attempt to maintain game face in the bright lights of summer fun collapsed into giggles and she couldn't help but flush in this rising humidity in the reading room with her and no I hadn't told my friends much, not mentioning us swimming naked in a thunderstorm as the rain poured and the dog stared at us, her ears down, waiting on the shoreline, and I didn't talk of how in the shower my index and pinkie fingers extended to reach from one nipple to the other flickering her into shivers and giggles again, or how she folded against me, arms wrapped around my waist while I'd feared that she compared my broad shoulders, thick thighs, rounded hips, and curved torso to that of skinny little Henry, all because of that one afternoon when her eyes gave her away, and her body froze on me, dry and dusty to touch, and what with the awkward hesitation, and a flash of a critical look between me and henry the night afterwards when we all sat and drank prosecco together on their porch, her on the wing with Henry, me in the one armchair, dog at my feet, cat on her lap, and I'd hated her then, so no, when my friends asked, how's it going, meaning she and I, they were curious naturally, surprised in a small way that I'd still been seeing her, hadn't left yet, and even though they had the timing down, knowing my patterns, a part of me wanted to blurt it all out, my fears, knowing the worst, remembering being scared enough to leave my home town as a kid, all because of not knowing how to date women even though I really wanted to, or thought I did, but once again, I didn't say a thing, held back, stored up these moments of connection and conversation, knowing it'd be over soon enough, and that there'll always be time to regret the choices we'd both silently taken, and so I told my friends, we're fine, lying.

Still Nervous, Rightly So

I remember another date on a Friday night. A rare kid free night. Clara had had to insist. Or so she told me. Describing how her friends, the ones she'd told about me, thought we weren't a good match, citing her marraige and well, how I was not a reliable or local man. Me? I was just happy she actually showed up at the tavern. I remember tapping my foot on the concrete floor, Steel Pulse blasting away overhead, and how we leaned in close to hear each other. My boots bounced in time with the drum and bass, heavy and hollow and she stared at me but I didn't get how annoying that was until she clamped a sandaled foot on top of mine. I gulped back my stout and dribbled a wee slurp down my tee shirt but the pattern hid the stain. Clara glanced around the room, nodding to a friend or two, then she stared at me and her lipstick was smeared across perfectly spaced front teeth. I leaned forward to wipe it off but my elbow landed in the tapas plate and when I jerked my arm out of there, I slapped her face, knocking off her fashionably expensive glasses which fell into my pint, spilling the rest of it onto her lap. Clara's nose bled. I pulled out an old cotton bandana from my back pocket—it was pretty clean—and reached for her left nostril. She smiled at me, I think, and took the hankie to mop up the beer from her jeans and then waved to the waiter for the bill.

Fear of Assimilation

No, no, no, I can't explain and she wouldn't understand even if I tried because Clara lives with her hubby and kid in a nice little corner Georgian house and she went to a nice private college for a business degree and even though she'd saved she still got into debt while she spent what three or four years at college living in a dorm and then in a sorority house and they had great wild parties there and her ex-boyfriends probably forced a few girls to go with them and that's rape by the way and I hope they didn't do that to her or fuck, well, too late now for me to stand up for Clara but anyway, then she left college for her first library job and a sensible cardigan and low heels in a shared office and then she got another promotion and then it carried on office to office and suit to suit and corner to corner and the more she earned the more she spent and the more she spent on newer stuff bigger houses fancier cars the more debt she got into and soon enough her kid's going to be looking at college options following in her and Henry's footsteps and there they are, both in debt, wanting to retire and she had all those dreams and she didn't do any of them because she didn't ask herself what she wanted because she'd followed the rules conventions jobs credit cards and they're about to get divorced and she'd like to settle with me, domesticate me, that's her hope, but it's too late because bang bang I'm done. I'm gone.

Last Chance at Being Publicly Awkward

The conversation didn't go as expected. Avoiding the topic of us, of Henry, or the kid, or her friends who no longer like me and all that messy stuff of a small town affair, we were talking about fashion and who gets to wear what. She'd picked up a glossy magazine as we'd waited for our table reservation, and nervously she checked out the room to see who she knew and more importantly who knew her, or that's what I imagined she did when she glanced past me and then back, with a sheepish grin. Once at our corner table, Clara folded her hands carefully over her lap, sensible Keens tapping on the floor. I tried to connect with her, keep us chatting, and so I threw out a few more questions about what she buys and why but then she asked me what was I thinking about—no, truly—and, even though she meant US, I couldn't go there, not now, not in her fancy local restaurant where everyone watched and judged and listened with eyes averted and conversations hushed, and so I told her: *In my twenties, tightywhities were my undies of choice. Family friendly, you could buy them anywhere, sexy too in the right context. In my thirties, I'd hang out in the back yard in boxers, striped boxers against a flat tanned stomach, and little else, perhaps a cowboy hat and boots if it were rattler season. Then came the sensible hip-huggers of my forties, cotton only, faded colours, flip flops, softer stomach, more sitting and less striding. At fifty though, what's next?* She knocked back her whiskey, stood up, grabbed her things and said, *depends.*

Broken

Clara. Clara. I uttered her name in the middle of the night as my dog snored on the pillow beside me. Clara, forgive me for my silent jealousy. Yes, this is your family, your husband and child, your hometown not mine. Remember dancing by the lake, those candles on the wooden table, walking through the woods, the red wine flowing from bottle to mouth, laughing as we stumbled across meadows and through the solitary corners of old town? We'd followed the stars above and the lights below, chasing our bare feet, desire falling silently from mouth to mouth, whispering and tasting you and the ham stuck in your teeth, no I didn't tell you, it was part of the charm, that one flaw, you needed an obvious flaw unlike my hidden ones, unexpected ones. My stealing. My leaving. You're returning. To him. Which came first? Does it even matter? Clara, can you forgive me for not being man enough?

Heading Out

Living there didn't work so well for me, not in a town like that, nestled in a valley, or rather buried alive in these trees and hills. Every action, comment or question asked of me drained. Last night, Clara wanted more. I couldn't give it. A commitment. A plan. A reason to leave Henry. To ask for a divorce. Fight, not our first. Tense dark eyes glowering at me as we stood in my kitchen, the sound of Henry's motorcycle stalling out in their yard and then silence. I knew better than to laugh, Henry was no biker, only a middle aged man feeling lost and alone. My dog grunted in her sleep. Clara waited on me. I knew I'd disappoint her again and again, that her family wouldn't accept me, want me, her kid would hate me and the sex, our desires and teases were already waxing and waning in the afternoon's patterns of storms and calm. I'd kept quiet. And then she'd stormed back next door. Quietly though. Don't wake the kid. Fuck. Again, I'm doing it again? When will I learn? Married women are taboo, deadly, don't go there, or so I should warn myself. The next morning, my mood worsened. It was time to leave, I told myself. The wind blew through the block and leaves fell, smothered me, with those low grey damp cardigan clouds and the noise of the radio, the bloody blathering DJs and newscasters, and oh, god, all that constant chatter, I couldn't stop it, shut it up, shut it out. It was another long Saturday stretching out in front of me and all I wanted was to walk away, or better yet, to close the door, open up the roof and fly away, up and over into the horizon, over the great lakes and into the Rockies, to sit high upon the peaks and open meadows, millions of acres of peace in front of me and no one knocking on my edges or needing anything from me but instead I was there in a rented home on a calm street with close—too close—neighbors and my fool heart clenched with every tree every shrub every leaf every car passing and then Clara's car drove past the window, happy families, all three of them laughing as music poured out her driver's window and I stood up to watch them turn the corner before walking next door to steal his bike.

***You stole his bike*, Clara said**

yes, I did
I wanted to break away,
smash the barrier of polite and awkward silence, both knowing but saying nothing about you, and I'd just wanted to get away like you had that day

> —Henry told me about bailing
> you out and the drive
> home when you
> mentioned us swimming
> naked at the lake.

yes, I did
I wanted him to know how much you like to play, and all on your terms, that there's more to you than the roles of wife and mother and cook and he agreed, telling me how much you like sex recently

> —He didn't threaten you,
> did he? Or did you
> threaten him?

Me? Oh no, no no, that's not me but he did say a few things that surprised me.

> —He told you that we're
> staying together, is that it?

Yes, he might have mentioned it.

> —He told me
> that you're not bad for a lesbian,
> no threat to him and me,
> he said, he loves me still

Yes, well...

                                    —Yes. Well. He said,
You. Are. Leaving.

Oh, he did? Well, I might have agreed to the idea

                                    —We need to talk,
Clara said,
I'm coming over, don't leave,
and she hung up.

White Lies and Alcohol

Pacifier in mouth (another beer that is), imaginary safety hardhat on, and in my own protection zone with the dog nearby, my boxes still packed, I was ready and there she was finally, Clara, my lover, former lover I suppose, and I put down the bottle and shed the cowboy hat and it made me sad but Clara said what she'd come to say and I hated all the pushing and the demanding and yes, she was just pushing me to listen because we both knew it's not really that we have to talk is it, no, she wanted to talk and she wanted me to say sorry for something, probably for being me and for not being Henry, the one before me, the one after me, the one she dreams about when alone or with me in the bed next to her, it didn't matter which and so I petted the dog and nodded along with the white lies and alcohol.

EPILOGUE

Down in the Dirt

Steaming hot strong coffee because it's too early in the morning but I'd wanted to get on the road before the sun baked the high desert hills. Summer heat creeps up with the smell of warm junipers in dry winds, and sunflowers in full yellow faces line the edges of these lonesome highways. Strangely shaped lava rocks line a four wheelin' track, rough and ready. I sleepily take in the mountains and birds and emptiness. The dog sticks her head out the open window, ears flapping. The bone rattling dirt road beyond Tent Rocks takes us up high into the Jemez Mountains, aiming for this one overlook worth seeing. That huge wealth of an untouched desert valley calms me. We head off further, beyond a gate that is locked for five months out of the year, up a rough track back in to the wildness of the Jemez, with creeks and meadows and tall evergreens, flowers, solitude, sun filled fields and open spaces I crave exploring with Clara. And I picture the day with us lazing in the tall native grasses and bright penstemons, eating bread and cheese, slowly talking and laughing and catching up on our dreams and adventures and endeavors and I am finally ready to tell her about my night terrors, why I keep moving, town to town, across the States, burning bridges, hiding in affairs and not relationships, and I want to confess my confusions and fears while soaking naked next to her in hidden hot springs. Instead I'm alone. Because I left with my dog and Clara stayed with Henry and I miss her. Her guilt and my shame.

Sarah **(sleam) Leamy** was a boring shy tomboy who suddenly left her English life and became a bit of a wanderer, street performer and writer. As a socially awkward and insecure Brit abroad, she lived first in Europe and then crossed the States and into Guatemala, performing, writing and working odd jobs as she explored new countries alone or with her dogs. She finally settled in New Mexico in her late twenties although she's still taking extended road trips when she can.

Sleam is the author of four award winning books, *When No One's Looking* (Eloquent Press), *Lucky Shot* (SBG), *Lucky Find* (Blue Mesa Books) and *Van Life*. Other work is (or soon to be) in *Los Angeles Review, Finishing Line Press, Hunger Mountain, Santa Fe Project Quarterly, Devil's Party Press, Dune Review,* and *Best Emerging Poets of NM* amongst others. She has just finished working on a new hybrid memoir, *Stay*, with Lidia Yuknavitch.

Sleam presents at various colleges and conferences on writing from a gender-queer perspective. She is passionate about sharing the importance, the craft, validation and conversation about representing outsider experiences through storytelling. She is a PhD researcher at the University of Birmingham, studying androgynous narratives in prose.

www.ingramcontent.com/pod-product-compliance
Lightning Source LLC
LaVergne TN
LVHW041507070426
835507LV00012B/1380